contents

2　6　8　10

13　16　18　20

22　25　28　30

For pattern inquiries, please visit: www.go-crafty.com

1

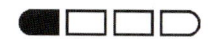

"C.L.E.A.N." nautical flag dishcloths

nautical dishcloth "C"

Yarn
Bernat® *Handicrafter*® *Cotton DeLux*™, 5oz/142g skeins, each approx 236yd/215m (cotton)
- 1 skein Navy #40040 (A)
- 1 skein Poppy Red #39950 (C)

Lily® *Sugar 'n Cream*® *Solids*, 2½oz/70g skeins, each approx 120yd/109m (cotton)
- 1 skein White #00001 (B)

Hook
- Size 7 (4.50mm) crochet hook *or size needed to obtain gauge*

Notions
- Tapestry needle

Finished Measurements
8½"/21.5 cm square.

Gauge
14 sts and 17 rows to 4"/10cm over sc.
Take time to check your gauge.

Dishcloth "C"
With A, ch 31.
Row 1 Sc in 2nd ch from hook and in each ch across. Ch 1, turn—30 sc.
Rows 2–5 Sc in each sc across. Ch 1, turn.
Row 6 Sc in each sc across. Change to B, ch 1, turn.
Rows 7–12 Rep Row 2.
Row 13 Sc in each sc across. Change to C, ch 1, turn—30 sc.
Rows 14–20 Rep Rows 7–13, changing to B at end of rep.
Rows 21–27 Rep Rows 7–13, changing to A at end of rep.
Rows 28–34 Rep Row 2. Do not end off.

Edging
Ch 1, turn work 90 degrees (¼ turn) clockwise, work 2 sc in corner, work 28 sc evenly spaced along side of dishcloth, (work 3 sc in corner, work 32 sc evenly spaced along next side of dishcloth) twice, work 1 more sc in corner. Join rnd with sl st in 1st sc. End off. Weave in ends.

nautical dishcloth "L"

Yarn
Bernat® *Handicrafter*® *Cotton DeLux*™, 5oz/142g skeins, each approx 236yd/215m (cotton)
- 1 skein Black #40016 (A)

Lily® *Sugar 'n Cream*®, 2½oz/70g skeins, each approx 120yd/109m (cotton)
- 1 skein Yellow #00010 (B)

Hook
- Size 7 (4.50mm) crochet hook *or size needed to obtain gauge*

Notions
- Tapestry needle

Finished Measurements
8½"/21.5 cm square.

Gauge
14 sts and 17 rows to 4"/10cm over sc.
Take time to check your gauge.

Dishcloth "L"
With A ch 15, change to B, ch 16 more.
Row 1 Sc in 2nd ch from hook and in each of next 14 ch, change to A, sc in each ch to end. Ch 1, turn—30 sc.
Row 2 Sc in each of 1st 15 sc, change to B, sc in each sc to end. Ch 1, turn.
Rows 3–16 Sc in each sc across, keeping color pattern as established (A on A sts, B on B sts).
Row 17 Sc in each of 1st 15 sc, change to A, sc in each sc to end. Change to B, ch 1, turn.
Row 18 Rep Row 2.
Rows 19–34 Sc in each sc across, keeping new color pattern as established. End off.

Edging
Work 1 rnd sc around dishcloth using A on A sts and B on B sts, placing 3 sc in each corner, and working 32 sc on each side, excluding corners. Join rnd with sl st in 1st sc. End off. Weave in ends.

nautical dishcloth "E"

Yarn
Bernat® *Handicrafter® Cotton DeLux™*, 5oz/142g skeins, each approx 236yd/215m (cotton)
- 1 skein Poppy Red #39950 (A)
- 1 skein Navy #40040 (B)

Hook
- Size 7 (4.50mm) crochet hook *or size needed to obtain gauge*

Notions
- Tapestry needle

Finished Measurements
8½"/21.5cm square.

Gauge
14 sts and 17 rows to 4"/10cm over sc.
Take time to check your gauge.

Dishcloth "E"
With A, ch 31.
Row 1 Sc in 2nd ch from hook and in each ch across. Ch 1, turn—30 sc.
Rows 2–16 Sc in each sc across. Ch 1, turn.
Row 17 Sc in each sc across. Change to B, ch 1, turn.
Rows 18–34 Rep Row 2. Do not end off.

Edging
Work 1 rnd sc around dishcloth using A on A sts and B on B sts, placing 3 sc in each corner, and having the same number of sc on each side (32 excluding corners). Join rnd with sl st in 1st sc. End off. Weave in ends.

nautical dishcloth "A"

Yarn
Lily® *Sugar 'n Cream® Solids*, 2½oz/70g skeins, each approx 120yd/109m (cotton)
- 1 skein White #00001 (A)

Bernat® *Handicrafter® Cotton DeLux™*, 5oz/142g skeins, each approx 236yd/215m (cotton)
- 1 skein Navy #40040 (B)

Hook
- Size 7 (4.50mm) crochet hook *or size needed to obtain gauge*

Notions
- 2 yarn bobbins for colorwork
- Tapestry needle

Finished Measurements
8½"/21.5 cm square.

Gauge
14 sts and 17 rows to 4"/10cm over sc.
Take time to check your gauge.

Notes
1 Use Invisible Float Color Change, illustrated on the inside back cover.
2 Wind one bobbin in A and one bobbin in B; use main skein for main section of A.

Dishcloth "A"
With A, ch 31.
Row 1 Sc in 2nd ch from hook and in each ch across. Ch 1, turn—30 sc.
Row 2 Sc in 1st 15 sc, change to B, sc each sc to end. Change to A, ch 1, turn.
Rows 3–31 Sc in each sc across following the chart on page 5 for color changes.

Edging
Ch 1, turn work 90 degrees (¼ turn) clockwise, work 2 sc in corner, work 29 sc evenly spaced along side of dishcloth, (work 3 sc in corner, work 29 sc evenly spaced along next side of dishcloth) twice, work 1 more sc in corner. Join rnd with sl st in 1st sc. End off. Weave in ends.

nautical dishcloth "N"

Yarn
Lily® *Sugar 'n Cream®* Solids, 2½oz/70g skeins, each approx 120yd/109m (cotton)
- 1 skein White #00001 (A)

Bernat® *Handicrafter®* Cotton DeLux™, 5oz/142g skeins, each approx 236yd/215m (cotton)
- 1 skein Navy #40040 (B)

Hook
- Size 7 (4.50mm) crochet hook *or size needed to obtain gauge*

Notions
- 4 yarn bobbins for colorwork
- Tapestry needle

Finished Measurements
8½"/21.5cm square.

Gauge
14 sts and 17 rows to 4"/10cm over sc.
Take time to check your gauge.

Notes
1 Use Invisible Float Color Change, illustrated on page 32.
2 Wind 2 bobbins in A and 2 bobbins in B.

Dishcloth "N"
With A ch 8, change to B, ch 7, change to A, ch 7, change to B, ch 9.
Row 1 Sc in 2nd ch from hook and in each of next 7 ch, with A sc in each of next 7 ch, with B sc in each of next 7 ch, with A sc in each of next 8 ch. Ch 1, turn—30 sc.
Rows 2–8 Sc in each sc across, working A on A sts and B on B sts. Ch 1, turn; at end of Row 8, change to A, ch 1, turn.
Row 9 Sc in each sc across, working A on B sts, and B on A sts. Ch 1, turn.
Rows 10–14 Rep Row 2.
Row 15 Sc in each sc across, working A on A sts and B on B sts. Ch 1, turn; at end of Row 15, change to A, ch 1, turn.
Rows 16–22 Rep Rows 9–15, changing to A at end of Row 22.
Rows 23–30 Rep Row 2. End off.

Edging
With B, work 1 rnd sc around dishcloth, placing 3 sc in each corner, and working 28 sc on each side, excluding corners. Join rnd with sl st in 1st sc. End off.
Weave in ends.

Nautical "A" Chart

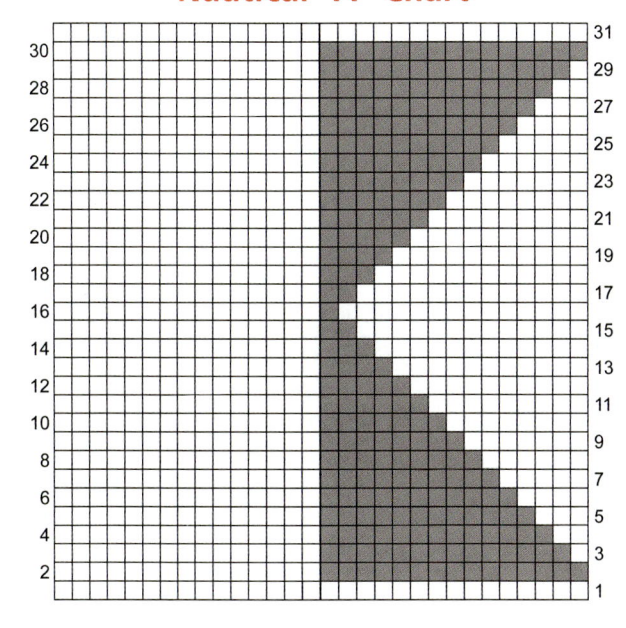

Color Key
☐ Color A
■ Color B

tulip

Yarn
Lily® *Sugar 'n Cream*® Scents, 3oz/85g skeins, each approx 150yd/138m (cotton)
- 1 skein Rose Petal #25046 (A)
- 1 skein Camomile #25010 (B)

Hook
- Size 7 (4.50mm) crochet hook *or size needed to obtain gauge*

Notions
- Straight or safety pins
- Tapestry needle

Finished Measurements
8"/20cm in diameter excluding flower center.

Gauge
14 sts and 8 rows to 4"/10cm over dc.
Take time to check your gauge.

Stitch Glossary
Dc5tog Double crochet 5 sts tog.
Picot Ch 3, sl st in 3rd ch from hook.

Note
Ch-3 counts as 1 dc throughout.

Flower
Base (make 2)
With A, ch 4 (counts as 1 dc).
Row 1 5 dc in 4th ch from hook. Ch 3, turn—6 dc.
Row 2 Dc in 1st dc, 2 dc in each dc across. Ch 3, turn—12 dc.
Row 3 Dc in 1st dc, dc in next dc, (2 dc in next dc, dc in next dc) 5 times. Ch 3, turn—18 dc.
Row 4 Dc in 1st dc, dc in each of next 2 dc, (2 dc in next dc, dc in each of next 2 dc) 5 times. Ch 3, turn—24 dc.
Row 5 Dc in 1st dc, dc in each of next 3 dc, (2 dc in next dc, dc in each of next 3 dc) 5 times. Ch 3, turn—30 dc.
Row 6 Dc in 1st dc, dc in each of next 4 dc, (2 dc in next dc, dc in each of next 4 dc) 5 times. Ch 3, turn—36 dc.
Row 7 Dc in 1st dc, dc in each of next 5 dc, (2 dc in next dc, dc in each of next 5 dc) 5 times. End off—42 dc.

Center
With B, ch 4.
Row 1 4 dc in 4th ch from hook. Ch 3, turn—5 dc.
Row 2 Dc in 1st dc, dc in each of next 3 dc, 2 dc in last dc. Ch 3 turn—7 dc.
Rows 3–4 Dc in 1st dc, dc in each dc across to last dc, 2 dc in last dc. Ch 3, turn—9 dc after Row 3; 11 dc after Row 4.
Rows 5–7 Dc2tog, dc in each dc across until 3 dc remain, dc2tog, dc in last dc. Ch 3, turn—9 dc after Row 5; 5 dc after Row 7.
Row 8 Dc5tog. Do not end off.

Center Edging
Continuing from Row 8, picot, sc evenly spaced around Center, picot. End off.

Base Edging and Assembly
With B, work sc evenly spaced across straight edge of 1st Base. End off. With B, work sc evenly spaced across straight edge of 2nd Base, 3 sc in corner, pin this Base on top of 1st Base at angle shown in photo, making sure Center fits neatly in the center, sc around entire curved edge of Flower, going through two layers where needed. Join rnd with sl st in 1st sc of 1st Base. End off.
Attach Center to assembled Base with B and whip st, so picots point up.
Weave in ends.

blue scrubby flower

Yarn
Lily® *Sugar 'n Cream®* Ombres, 2oz/56g skeins, each approx 95yd/86m (cotton)
- 1 skein Swimming Pool #02744

Hook
- Size 7 (4.50mm) crochet hook *or size needed to obtain gauge*

Notions
- Blue plastic pot scrubber
- Stitch marker
- Tapestry needle

Finished Measurements
8"/20cm in diameter including edging.

Gauge
16 sts and 16 rows to 4"/10cm over sc.
Take time to check your gauge.

Stitch Glossary
Scflo Single crochet in the front loop.

Note
First rnd of sc is worked directly into the scrubby by inserting hook down through 2–3 layers of plastic mesh, then up through those layers ¼"/.5cm or so ahead of where the hook went down. Yo, pull through mesh, yo, pull through 2 loops on hook as for regular sc. For extra stability, start each consecutive st by going down into the mesh in the same spot as the previous st came up.

Scrubby
Rnd 1 Work 30 sc evenly spaced around center edge of scrubby. Join rnd with sl st in flo of 1st sc, ch 1.

Inner Petal 1
Row 1 Sc in flo of same sc as sl st, scflo in each of next 5 sc. Ch 1, turn—6 sc.
Row 2 Sc in each sc across. Ch 1, turn.
Row 3 2 sc in 1st sc, sc in each of next 4 sc, 2 sc in last sc. Ch 1, turn—8 sc.
Row 4 Rep Row 2.
Row 5 Sc2tog, sc in each of next 4 sc, sc2tog. Ch 1, turn—6 sc.
Row 6 Sc2tog, sc in each of next 2 sc, sc2tog. Ch 1, turn—4 sc.
Row 7 Sc2tog twice. Ch 1, turn.
Row 8 Sc2tog. End off.

Inner Petals 2–5
Row 1 Join yarn with scflo in next sc of Rnd 1 of Scrubby, scflo in each of next 5 sc. Ch 1, turn— 6 sc.
Rep Rows 2–8 of Inner Petal 1.

Outer Petals (make 5)
Outer Petals are worked the same as Inner Petals except they are worked in back loop only of Rnd 1 of Scrubby, using 3 sc behind the left side of any Petal and 3 sc behind the right side of the next Petal.

Edging (work once on Inner Petals and once on Outer Petals)
Rnd 1 Sc evenly around entire edge, working sc2tog at base of each petal where it meets its neighbor, 2 sc in each side point at the increases, and 3 sc in each top point. Join rnd with sl st in 1st sc. End off.
Weave in ends.

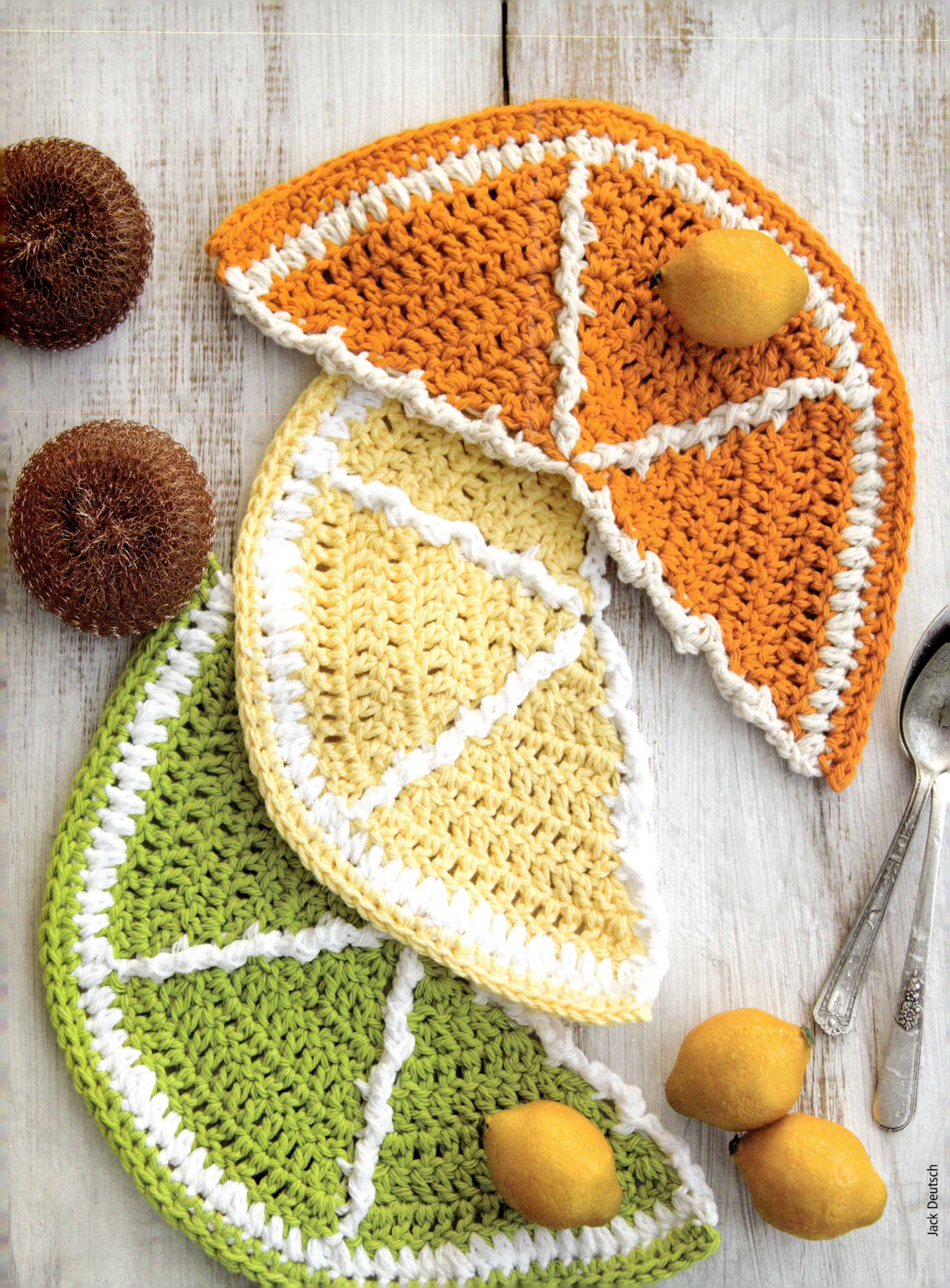

Jack Deutsch

citrus dishcloths

Yarn
Lily® Sugar 'n Cream® Solids, 2½oz/70g skeins, each approx 120yd/109m (cotton)
- 1 skein Yellow #00010 (A), OR
- 1 skein Hot Green #01712 (A)
- 1 skein White #00001 (B) for lemon or lime dishcloths

Lion Brand® Kitchen Cotton, 2oz/57g skeins each approx 99yd/90m (cotton)
- 1 skein Pumpkin #133 (A)
- 1 skein Vanilla #098 (B) for orange dishcloth

Hook
- Size 7 (4.50mm) crochet hook *or size needed to obtain gauge*

Notions
- 7 yarn bobbins for colorwork
- Tapestry needle

Finished Measurements
12"/30.5cm across at widest point x 5½"/14cm tall at tallest point.

Gauge
12 sts and 8 rows to 4"/10cm over dc.
Take time to check your gauge.

Notes
1 Ch-3 does not count as st after Row 1.
2 Before you begin, wind 7 bobbins; 3 A and 4 B.

Stitch Glossary
Fptr (front post treble crochet) On RS row, work a treble crochet around the post of designated st instead of through its loops. Yo twice, insert hook from front to back to front around post, yo, draw through st, (yo, draw through two loops on hook) 3 times.
Bptr (back post treble crochet) On WS Row, work as for Fptr but insert hook from back to front to back.
Puff st (Yo, insert hook in designated st, yo, draw through st) 3 times, yo draw through 6 loops on hook, yo draw through 2 loops on hook.

Dishcloth
With B, ch 4.
Row 1 Change to A, dc in 4th ch from hook, change to B, dc in same ch, (change to A, dc in same ch, change to B, dc in same ch) twice. Ch 3, turn—7 dc (4 B and 3 A).
Row 2 Bptr around 1st dc, (change to A, 3 dc in next dc, change to B, Bptr around next dc) 3 times. Ch 3, turn—4 Bptr and 9 dc (ch-3 does not count as st here and for all remaining rows).
Row 3 Fptr around 1st Bptr, (change to A, 2 dc in next dc, dc around next dc, 2 dc in next dc, change to B, Fptr around next Bptr) 3 times. Ch 3, turn—4 Fptr and 15 dc.
Row 4 Bptr around 1st Fptr, (change to A, 2 dc in next dc, dc in each of next 3 dc, 2 dc in next dc, change to B, Bptr around next Fptr) 3 times. Ch 3, turn—4 Bptr and 21 dc.
Rows 5–8 Continue in pattern as established, working 2 dc in both end sts of each segment in A, with 2 more dc between them on every row, and a post st around every post st in B. Ch 2, turn after Row 8—4 Fptr and 45 dc at end of Row 8. End off all bobbins.
Row 9 With RS facing and B, (puff st in each of 5 sts, 2 puff sts in next st) twice, puff st in each of 9 sts, 2 puff sts in next st, puff st in each of 5 sts, 2 puff sts in next st, puff st in each of 9 sts, 2 puff sts in next st, puff st in each of 5 sts, 2 puff sts in next st, puff st in each st to end. Change to A, ch 1, turn—55 puff sts.
Row 10 Sc in 1st st, 2 sc in next st, (sc in each of next 15 sts, 2 sc in next st, sc in next st, 2 sc in next st) twice, sc in each of next 15 sts, 2 sc in next st, sc in last st. Ch 1, turn—61 sc.
Row 11 Sl st in each sc across to end. End off. Weave in ends.

Jack Deutsch

wide rainbow log cabin

Yarn
Lion Brand® *Kitchen Cotton*, 2oz/57g skeins each approx 99yd/90m (cotton)
- 1 skein Pumpkin #133 (A)
- 1 skein Bubble Gum #103 (B)
- 1 skein Grape #147 (C)
- 1 skein Tropic Breeze #148 (D)
- 1 skein Snap Pea #130 (E)

Hook
- Size 7 (4.50mm) crochet hook *or size needed to obtain gauge*

Notions
- Stitch marker
- Tapestry needle

Finished Measurements
8"/20cm square including edging.

Gauge
8"/20cm square including edging.
Take time to check your gauge.

Dishcloth
Center
With A, ch 6.
Row 1 (RS) Sc in 2nd ch from hook and in each ch across. Ch 1, turn—5 sc.
Rows 2–5 Sc in each sc across. Ch 1, turn. End off after Row 5.

First Strip
Turn work ¼ turn clockwise. With RS facing join B with sl st in right corner of Center, ch 1.
Row 1 Work 5 sc evenly spaced across side of Center. Ch 1, turn—5 sc.
Rows 2–3 Sc in each sc across. Ch 1, turn.
Row 4 Sc in 1st sc, place marker in side of st just made, sc in each sc across. End off.

Second Strip
Turn work ¼ turn clockwise. With RS facing join C with sl st at marker, ch 1. Remove marker.
Row 1 Work 9 sc evenly spaced across: 4 across side of B rows, 1 sc in opposite side of foundation ch of each sc of Center. Ch 1, turn—9 sc.
Rows 2–3 Sc in each sc across. Ch 1, turn.
Row 4 Sc in 1st sc, place marker in side of st just made, sc in each sc across. End off.

Third Strip
Turn work ¼ turn clockwise. With RS facing join D with sl st at marker, ch 1. Remove marker.
Row 1 Work 9 sc evenly spaced across. Ch 1, turn—9 sc.
Rows 2–3 Sc in each sc across. Ch 1, turn.
Row 4 Sc in 1st sc, place marker in side of st just made, sc in each sc across. End off.

Fourth Strip
Turn work ¼ turn clockwise. With RS facing join E with sl st at marker, ch 1. Remove marker.
Row 1 Work 13 sc evenly spaced across: 4 across side of D rows, 1 sc in each sc of Center, 4 across side of B rows. Ch 1, turn—13 sc.
Rows 2–3 Sc in each sc across. Ch 1, turn.
Row 4 Sc in 1st sc, place marker in side of st just made, sc in each sc across. End off.

Fifth Strip
Turn work ¼ turn clockwise. With RS facing join A with sl st at marker, ch 1. Remove marker.
Rows 1–4 Rep Rows 1–4 of Fourth Strip. Continue on in this manner, working each strip at a 90 degree angle to the strip before, maintaining color pattern in A, B, C, D, E, and working 4 more sc along each strip, until dishcloth is just under 8"/20 cm square, ending with a strip in C.

Edging
With A, work 1 rnd sc evenly spaced around, placing 3 sc in each corner. Join rnd with sl st in 1st sc. End off.
Weave in ends.

skinny rainbow log cabin

Yarn
Lion Brand® *Kitchen Cotton*, 2oz/57g skeins each approx 99yd/90m (cotton)
- 1 skein Pumpkin #133 (A)
- 1 skein Bubble Gum #103 (B)
- 1 skein Grape #147 (C)
- 1 skein Tropic Breeze #148 (D)
- 1 skein Snap Pea #130 (E)

Hook
- Size 7 (4.50mm) crochet hook *or size needed to obtain gauge*

Notions
- Stitch marker
- Tapestry needle

Finished Measurements
8"/20cm square including edging.

Gauge
8"/20cm square including edging.
Take time to check your gauge.

Dishcloth
Center
With A, ch 6.
Row 1 (RS) Sc in 2nd ch from hook and in each ch across. Ch 1, turn—5 sc.
Rows 2–5 Sc in each sc across. Ch 1, turn. End off after Row 5.

First Strip
Turn work ¼ turn clockwise. With RS facing join B with sl st in right corner of Center, ch 1.
Row 1 Work 5 sc evenly spaced across side of Center. Ch 1, turn—5 sc.
Row 2 Sc in 1st sc, place marker in side of st just made, sc in each sc across. End off.

Second Strip
Turn work ¼ turn clockwise. With RS facing join C with sl st at marker, ch 1. Remove marker.
Row 1 Work 7 sc evenly spaced across; 2 sc across side of B rows, 1 sc in opposite side of foundation ch of each sc of Center. Ch 1, turn—7 sc.
Row 2 Sc in 1st sc, place marker in side of st just made, sc in each sc across. End off.

Third Strip
Turn work ¼ turn clockwise. With RS facing join D with sl st at marker, ch 1. Remove marker.
Row 1 Work 7 sc evenly spaced across. Ch 1, turn—7 sc.
Row 2 Sc in 1st sc, place marker in side of st just made, sc in each sc across. End off.

Fourth Strip
Turn work ¼ turn clockwise. With RS facing join E with sl st at marker, ch 1. Remove marker.
Row 1 Work 9 sc evenly spaced across; 2 sc across side of D rows, 1 sc in each sc of Center, 2 sc across side of B rows. Ch 1, turn—9 sc.
Row 2 Sc in 1st sc, place marker in side of st just made, sc in each sc across. End off.

Fifth Strip
Turn work ¼ turn clockwise. With RS facing join A with sl st at marker, ch 1. Remove marker.
Rows 1–2 Rep Rows 1–2 of Fourth Strip. Continue on in this manner, working each strip at a 90 degree angle to the strip before, maintaining color pattern in A, B, C, D, E, and working 2 more sc along each strip, until dishcloth is just under 8"/20 cm square, ending with a strip in E.

Edging
With C, work 1 rnd sc evenly spaced around, placing 3 sc in each corner. Join rnd with sl st in 1st sc. End off.
Weave in ends.

soapy owl dishcloth

Yarn
Lily® Sugar 'n Cream® Ombres, 2oz/56g skeins, each approx 95yd/86m (cotton)
- 1 skein Earth Ombre #02046 (A)

Bernat® Handicrafter® Cotton DeLux™, 5oz/142g skeins, each approx 236yd/215m (cotton),
- 1 skein Espresso #40032 (B)

Lily® Sugar 'n Cream® Solids, 2½oz/70g skeins, each approx 120yd/10m (cotton)
- 1 skein White #00001 (C)
- Small amounts black and orange cotton yarn

Hook
- Size 7 (4.50mm) crochet hook *or size needed to obtain gauge*

Notions
- Stitch marker
- Tapestry needle

Finished Measurements
8"/20 cm across at widest point x 10"/25 cm tall.

Gauge
8 rnds to 4"/10cm over sc.
Take time to check your gauge.

Notes
1 Ch-3 counts as 1 dc throughout.
2 Rnds 1–9 are worked in a spiral; mark 1st st of each rnd to keep track.

Scarf
Body
With A, ch 2.
Rnd 1 6 sc in 2nd ch from hook.
Rnd 2 2 sc in each sc around—12 sc.
Rnd 3 (2 sc in next sc, sc in next sc) 6 times—18 sc.
Rnd 4 (2 sc in next sc, sc in each of next 2 sc) 6 times—24 sc.
Rnd 5 (2 sc in next sc, sc in each of next 3 sc) 6 times—30 sc.
Rnd 6 (2 sc in next sc, sc in each of next 4 sc) 6 times—36 sc.
Rnd 7 (2 sc in next sc, sc in each of next 5 sc) 6 times—42 sc.
Rnd 8 (2 sc in next sc, sc in each of next 6 sc) 6 times—48 sc.
Rnd 9 (2 sc in next sc, sc in each of next 7 sc) 6 times—54 sc.
Rnd 10 Change to B, ch 3, dc in first sc, dc in each of next 3 sc, 2 dc in next sc, dc in each of next 4 sc, *2 dc in next sc, dc in each of next 3 dc, 2 dc in next dc, dc in each of next 4 sc. Rep from * around. Join rnd with sl st in top of beg ch-3—66 dc.

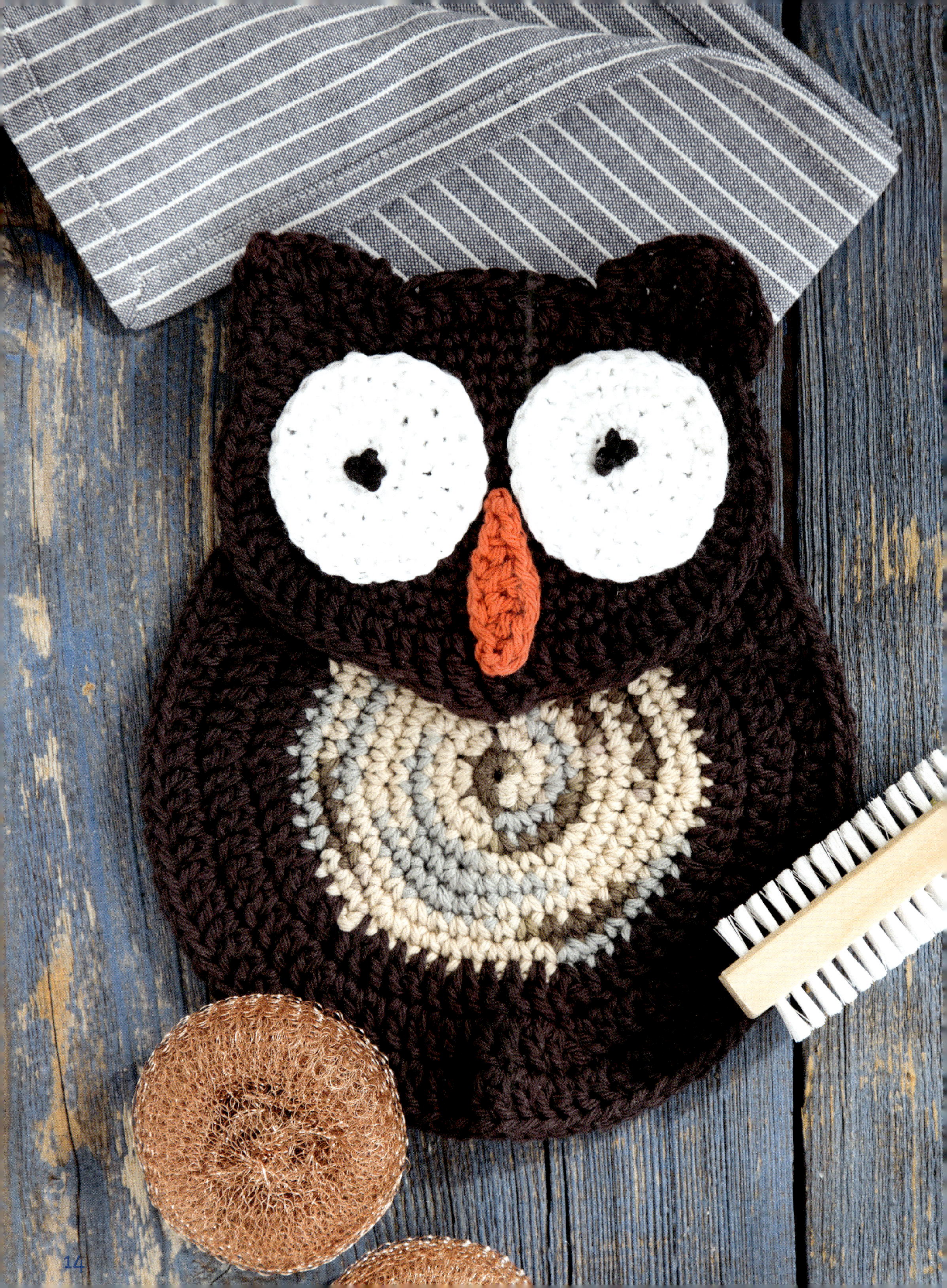

soapy owl dishcloth

Rnd 11 Ch 3, dc in first dc, dc in each of next 4 dc, 2 dc in next dc, dc in each of next 5 dc, *2 dc in next dc, dc in each of next 4 dc, 2 dc in next dc, dc in each of next 5 dc. Rep from * around. Join rnd with sl st in top of beg ch-3—78 dc.

Rnd 12 Change to B, ch 3, dc in first dc, dc in each of next 5 dc, 2 dc in next dc, dc in each of next 6 dc, *2 dc in next dc, dc in each of next 5 dc, 2 dc in next dc, dc in each of next 6 dc. Rep from * around until 13 sts remain. Leave remaining sts unworked—75 dc. End off.

Head

With B, ch 6.

Rnd 1 3 sc in 2nd ch from hook, sc in each of next 3 ch, 4 sc in next ch, sc in each of next 4 ch on opposite side of foundation ch. Join rnd with sl st in 1st sc—14 sc.

Rnd 2 Ch 1, 2 sc in each of 1st 3 sc, sc in each of next 4 sc, 2 sc in each of next 3 sc, sc in each of next 4 sc. Join rnd with sl st in 1st sc—20 sc.

Rnd 3 Ch 1, 2 sc in 1st sc, (sc in next sc, 2 sc in next sc) twice, sc in each of next 5 sc, (2 sc in next sc, sc in next sc) 3 times, sc in each of next 4 sc. Join rnd with sl st in 1st sc—26 sc.

Rnd 4 Ch 1, 2 sc in 1st sc, (sc in each of next 2 sc, 2 sc in next sc) twice, sc in each of next 6 sc, 2 sc in next sc, (sc in each of next 2 sc, 2 sc in next sc) twice, sc in each of next 6 sc. Join rnd with sl st in 1st sc—32 sc.

Rnd 5 Ch 1, 2 sc in 1st sc, (sc in each of next 3 sc, 2 sc in next sc) twice, sc in each of next 7 sc, 2 sc in next sc, (sc in each of next 3 sc, 2 sc in next sc) twice, sc in each of next 7 sc. Join rnd with sl st in 1st sc—38 sc.

Rnd 6 Ch 1, 2 sc in 1st sc, (sc in each of next 4 sc, 2 sc in next sc) twice, sc in each of next 8 sc, 2 sc in next sc, (sc in each of next 4 sc, 2 sc in next sc) twice, sc in each of next 8 sc. Join rnd with sl st in 1st sc—44 sc.

Rnd 7 Ch 1, 2 sc in 1st sc, (sc in each of next 5 sc, 2 sc in next sc) twice, sc in each of next 9 sc, 2 sc in next sc, (sc in each of next 5 sc, 2 sc in next sc) twice, sc in each of next 9 sc. Join rnd with sl st in 1st sc—50 sc.

Rnd 8 Ch 3, dc in 1st sc, (dc in each of next 2 sc, 2 dc in next sc) 5 times, dc in each of next 4 sc, tr in each of next 3 sc, dc in each of next 3 sc, 2 dc in next sc, (dc in each of next 2 sc, 2 dc in next sc) 5 times, dc in each of next 10 sc. Join rnd with sl st in top of beg ch-3. End off—59 dc and 3 tr.

First Ear

Orient Head so the tr sts are pointing down for the chin. Place marker in sc at top of head, opposite center of chin. Count 10 sts to the right of marked st, join B with sc in that st.

Row 1 Hdc in next sc, dc in next dc, tr in next dc, dc in next dc, hdc in next dc, sc in next dc. Turn.

Row 2 Sl st in 1st st, sc in next st, hdc in next st, (dc, tr, dc) in next st, hdc in next st, sc in next st, sl st in next st. End off.

Second Ear

Skip 3 dc after marked dc, join B with sc in next sc.

Rep Rows 1–2 of First Ear.

Eyes (make 2)

With C, work Rnds 1–4 of Body. Join rnd with sl st in 1st sc. End off, leaving long tail with which to sew.

Beak

With orange, ch 9.

Row 1 Sl st in 2nd ch from hook, sc in next ch, hdc in next ch, dc in next ch, tr in next ch, dc in next ch, hdc in next ch, sc in next ch. End off, leaving a long tail with which to sew.

Finishing

With B, sew Head to Body, orienting Head so that tr chin points down, and the opening in Rnd 11 of Body is covered.

With C, sew Eyes to Head with a whip st.

With Black, embroider 3 French knots in the center of each eye.

Orient Beak so the narrow side is pointing up between the eyes. Sew it into place.

Weave in ends. ■

Jack Deutsch

natural shells

Yarn
Lion Brand® *Kitchen Cotton*, 2oz/57g skeins each approx 99yd/90m (cotton)
- 1 skein Vanilla #098

Hook
- Size 7 (4.50mm) crochet hook *or size needed to obtain gauge*

Notions
- Tapestry needle

Finished Measurements
8"/20cm square including edging.

Gauge
16 sts and 14 rows to 4"/10cm over pattern st.
Take time to check your gauge.

Dishcloth
Ch 30.
Row 1 Sc in 2nd ch from hook, sk 1 ch, 3 sc in next ch, *sk 2 ch, 3 sc in next ch. Rep from* until 2 ch remain, sk 1 ch, sc in last ch. Ch 1, turn—9 3-sc shells and 2 sc.
Row 2 Sc in 1st sc, sk 1 sc, 3 sc in next sc, *sk 2 sc, 3 sc in next sc. Rep from * across, sk 1 sc, sc in last sc. Ch 1, turn.
Rep Row 2 for pattern until work measures 7¾"/19.5cm. Do not end off.

Edging
Work 2 more sc into sc just made for corner, 3 sc in every other row end across, 3 sc in corner, working opposite side of foundation ch, work 3 sc in base of each 3-sc shell, 3 sc in corner, 3 sc in every other row end, 2 sc 1st sc of last row for corner. Join rnd with sl st in 1st sc. End off. Weave in ends.

SYMBOL KEY
- ○ ch
- † sc
- ⊥ 3 sc in same st

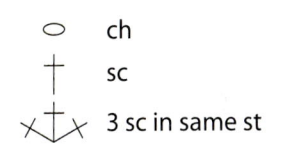

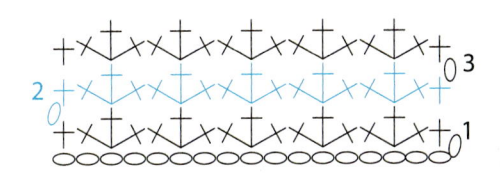

natural ridges

Yarn
Lion Brand® *Kitchen Cotton*, 2oz/57g skeins each approx 99yd/90m (cotton)
- 1 skein Vanilla #098

Hook
- Size 7 (4.50mm) crochet hook *or size needed to obtain gauge*

Notions
- Tapestry needle

Finished Measurements
8"/20cm square including edging.

Gauge
16 sts and 16 rows to 4"/10cm over scblo.
Take time to check your gauge.

Stitch Glossary
Scblo Single crochet in back loop only.

Dishcloth
Ch 31.
Row 1 Sc in 2nd ch from hook and in each ch across. Ch 1, turn—30 sc.
Row 2 Scblo in each sc across. Ch 1, turn.
Rep Row 2 for pattern until work measures 7¾"/19.5cm. End off.

Edging
Work 1 rnd sc evenly spaced around, placing 3 sc in each corner. Join rnd with sl st in 1st sc. End off.
Weave in ends.

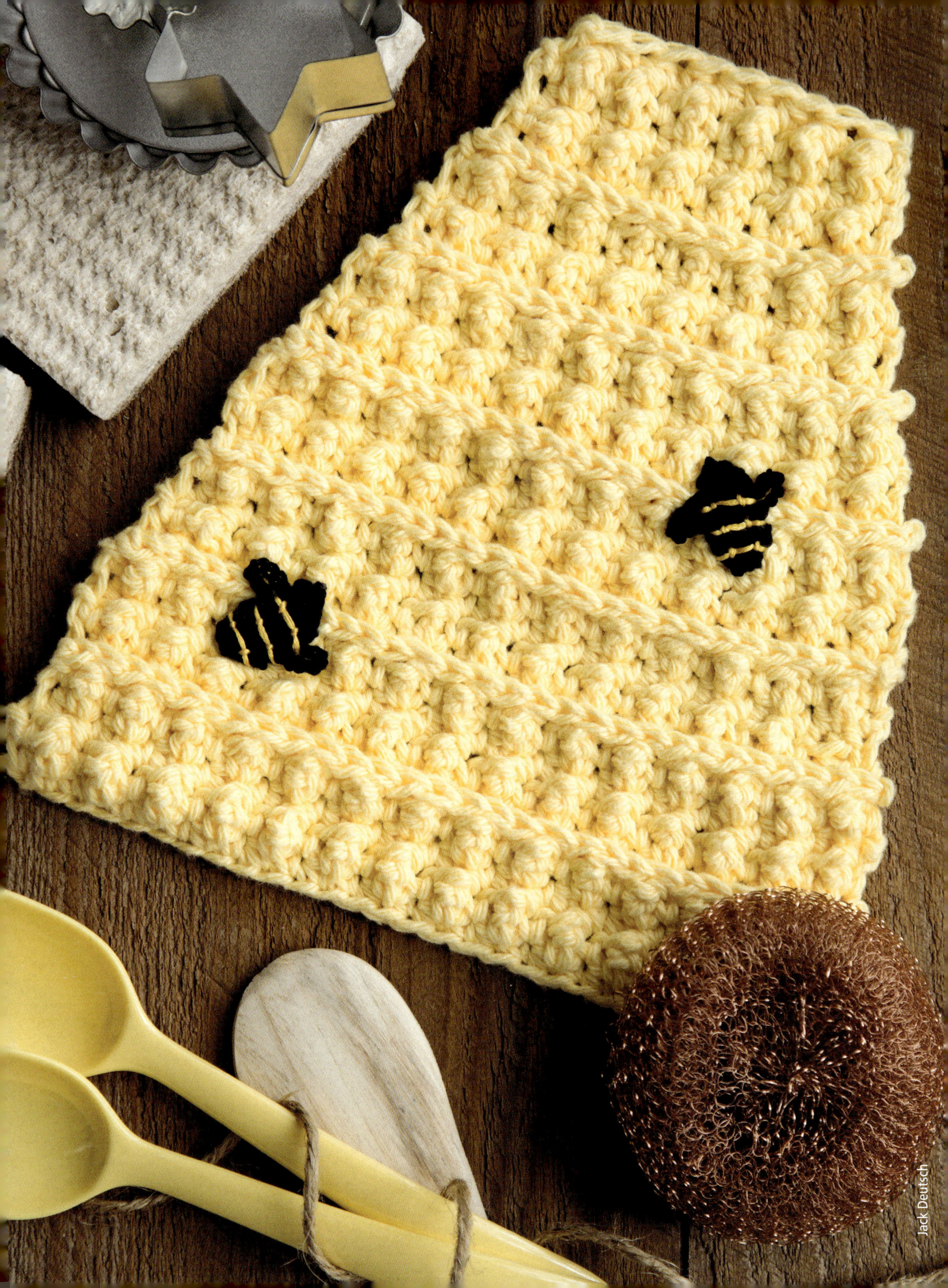
Jack Deutsch

beehive dishcloth

Yarn
Lily® *Sugar 'n Cream*® *Solids*, 2½oz/70g skeins, each approx 120yd/109m (cotton)
- 1 skein Yellow #00010 (A)
- Small amount of size 3 black crochet thread (B
- Small amount of yellow embroidery floss

Hooks
- Size 7 (4.50mm) crochet hook *or size needed to obtain gauge*
- B/1 (2.25mm) crochet hook

Notions
- Tapestry needle
- Embroidery needle

Finished Measurements
8"/20cm tall by 8"/20cm at base.

Gauge
15 sts and 14 rows to 4"/10cm over pattern st using size 7 (4.50mm) hook.
Take time to check your gauge.

Stitch Glossary
Scblo Single crochet in the back loop only.
Sc3tog (Single crochet 3 together) (Insert hook into next st, yo and draw up a lp) in next 3 sts. Yo and draw through all four lps on hook—2 sts dec.

Notes
1 Ch-3 counts as 1 dc throughout.
2 Shell = 3 dc in designated st.

Dishcloth
With A and larger hook, ch 30.
Row 1 (RS) Sc in 2nd ch from hook and in each ch across. Ch 1, turn—29 sc.
Row 2 (WS) Sc in 1st sc, * tr in next sc, sc in next sc. Rep from * to end. Ch 1, turn.
Row 3 Sc in each st across. Ch 1, turn.
Row 4 Rep Row 2.
Row 5 Scblo in each st across. Ch 1, turn.
Rows 6–9 Rep Rows 2–5.
Row 10 Sl st in 1st sc, sc2tog, tr in next sc, *sc in next sc, tr in next sc. Rep from * across until 3 sts remain, sc2tog, leave last st unworked. Ch 1, turn—25 sts.
Rows 11–13 Rep Rows 3–5.
Row 14–17 Rep Rows 2–5.
Rows 18–28 Rep Rows 10–13 twice, then Rows 10–12 once more—13 sts.
Row 29 Sc in each of 1st 3 sts, hdc in each of next 7 sts, sc in each of last 3 sts. End off.

Bees (make 2 or more)
With B and smaller hook, ch 2.
Row 1 3 sc in 2nd ch from hook. Ch 1, turn—3 sc.
Row 2 Sc in each sc across. Ch 1, turn.
Rows 3 and 4 Sc in each sc across. Ch 7, turn.
Row 5 Rep Row 2.
Row 6 Sc3tog. End off.

Finishing
With A and larger hook, sl st across front loops of each scblo row.
With yellow embroidery floss, embroider bee stripes as shown in photo.
Stitch bees to beehive as shown in photo.
Weave in ends.

Jack Deutsch

elephant dishcloth

Yarn
Lily® Sugar 'n Cream® Solids, 2½oz/70g skeins, each approx 120yd/109m (cotton),
- 1 skein Rose Pink #00046
- Small amount of black cotton for eye

Hook
- Size 7 (4.50mm) crochet hook *or size needed to obtain gauge*

Notions
- Straight or safety pins
- Tapestry needle

Finished Measurements
7"/18cm at widest point excluding trunk x 7"/18cm at tallest point.

Gauge
12 sts and 8 rows to 4"/10cm over dc.
Take time to check your gauge.

Elephant
Body
Ch 9.
Row 1 Dc in 4th ch from hook and in each of next 4 ch, 5 dc in last ch, working up the opposite side of foundation ch, dc in each ch to end. Ch 3, turn—17 dc.
Row 2 Dc in each of next 5 dc, 2 dc in next dc, dc in next dc, 3 dc in next dc, dc in next dc, 2 dc in next dc, dc in each dc to end. Ch 3, turn—21 dc.
Row 3 Dc in each of next 5 dc, 2 dc in next dc, dc in each of next 3 dc, 3 dc in next dc, dc in each of next 3 dc, 2 dc in next dc, dc in each dc to end. End off—25 dc.
Row 4 Turn work, ch 6 (for leg), dc in top of last dc made in Row 3 and in each of next 6 dc, 2 dc in next dc, dc in each of next 4 dc, 3 dc in next dc, dc in each of next 4 dc, 2 dc in next dc, dc in each dc to end, ch 8, turn—29 dc and 14 ch.
Row 5 Dc in 4th ch from hook and in each of next 4 ch, dc in next 8 dc, 2 dc in next dc, dc in next 5 dc, (dc, ch 1, dc) in next dc, dc in next 5 dc, 2 dc in next dc, dc in next 8 dc, dc in last 6 ch. Ch 3, turn—44 dc.
Row 6 Dc in each of 15 dc, ch 9, sl st in 2nd ch from hook and in each ch across, back to regular row (tail made), dc in same st as last dc, dc in next 6 dc, 3 dc in ch-1 sp, dc in next 6 dc, 2 dc in next dc, dc in each dc to end. End off—49 dc and tail.

Body Edging
Join yarn on belly at one leg, sc across evenly to other leg. End off.

Head
Ch 4.
Rnd 1 11 dc in 4th ch from hook. Join rnd with sl st in top of beg-ch—12 dc (ch-3 counts as 1 dc here and throughout).
Rnd 2 Ch 3, dc in 1st dc, 2 dc in each dc around. Join rnd with sl st in top of beg-ch—24 dc.
Rnd 3 Ch 3, dc in 1st dc, dc in next dc, *2 dc in next dc, dc in next dc. Rep from * around. Join rnd with sl st in top of beg-ch—36 dc.

Ear
Row 1 Ch 3, turn, dc in same st as sl st, dc in each of next 5 dc, 2 dc in next dc. Ch 3, turn—9 dc.
Row 2 Dc in 1st dc, dc each dc across to last dc, 2 dc in last dc. Ch 3, turn—11 dc.
Row 3 Rep Row 2. End off—13 dc.

Trunk
Ch 12.
Row 1 Tr in 5th ch from hook and in each of next 2 ch, 3 tr in next ch, tr in each ch to end. End off—11 tr.

Finishing
With Black, embroider French knot for eye. Stitch Trunk to Head as shown in photo. Stitch Head to Body at angle shown in photo. Weave in ends.

Jack Deutsch

house dishcloth

Yarn
Bernat® Handicrafter® Cotton DeLux™, 5oz/142g skeins, each approx 236yd/215m (cotton)
- 1 skein Morning Glory #40008 (A)
- 1 skein Paprika #39968 (B)
- 1 skein Purple #39976 (C)
- 1 skein Espresso #40032 (D)

Hook
- Size 7 (4.50mm) crochet hook *or size needed to obtain gauge*

Notions
- 6 yarn bobbins for colorwork
- Tapestry needle

Finished Measurements
9"/23cm wide at widest point x 7¾"/20cm tall at tallest point.

Gauge
14 sts and 17 rows to 4"/10cm over sc.
Take time to check your gauge.

Note
Wind 6 bobbins: 3 A, 1 B and 2 C.

Stitch Glossary
Picot Ch 3, sl st in 3rd ch from hook.

Dishcloth
House
With A ch 11, change to B ch 7, change to A ch 12.
Row 1 Sc in 2nd ch from hook and in each of next 10 ch, with B sc in each of next 7 ch, with A sc in each of next 11 ch. Ch 1, turn—29 sc.
Row 2 Sc in each of 1st 11 sc, with B sc in each of next 7 sc, with A sc in each of last 11 sc. Ch 1, turn.
Rows 3–11 Rep Row 2.
Rows 12 and 13 With A, sc in each sc across. Ch 1, turn.
Row 14 Sc in each of 1st 4 sc, with C, sc in each of next 5 sc, with A, sc in each of next 11 sc, with C, sc in each of next 5 sc, with A sc in each of next 4 sc. Ch 1, turn.
Rows 15–18 Rep Row 14.
Rows 19–24 With A, sc in each sc across. Ch 1, turn. End off after Row 24.

Roof
With D, ch 32.
Row 1 Sc in 2nd ch from hook and in each ch across. Ch 3, turn—31 sc.
Row 2 (RS) (Dc, picot, 2 dc) in 1st sc, [sk 2 sc, sc in next sc, sk 2 sc, (2 dc, picot, 2 dc) in next dc] 5 times. End off.
Turn work over to stitch in opposite side of foundation ch. Join yarn with sl st in base of 1st sc, ch 3.
Row 1 Dc2tog, dc in base of each sc across until 3 sts remain, dc2tog, dc in last sc. Ch 3, turn—29 dc.
Row 2 Dc2tog, dc in each dc across until 3 sts remain, dc2tog, dc in last dc. Ch 3, turn—27 dc.
Rows 3 and 4 Rep Row 2. End off after Row 4—23 dc after Row 4.

Roof Edging
With RS facing and D, work 1 row sc evenly spaced from lower right corner around top of roof to lower left coner, placing 3 sc in each upper corner. End off.

Finishing
With D, whip stitch Roof to House, making sure Roof trim overlaps top of House as shown in photo.
With B, embroider running st around door as shown in photo.
With C, make 1 French knot for a doorknob as shown in photo.
Weave in ends.

'60s van dishcloth

Yarn
Lion Brand® Kitchen Cotton, 2oz/57g skeins each approx 99yd/90m (cotton)
- 1 skein Snap Pea #130 (A)
- 1 skein Citrus #157 (B)
- 1 skein Bubble Gum #103 (C)
- 1 skein Vanilla #98 (D)
- 1 skein Licorice #153 (E)

Hook
- Size 7 (4.50mm) crochet hook *or size needed to obtain gauge*

Notions
- 5 yarn bobbins for colorwork
- Tapestry needle

Finished Measurements
9¼"/23.5cm wide at widest point x 8½"/22cm tall at tallest point excluding wheels.

Gauge
14 sts and 17 rows to 4"/10cm over sc.
Take time to check your gauge.

Note
Wind 5 bobbins: 3 C and 2 D.

Stitch Glossary
Scblo Single crochet in the back loop only.
Sc3tog (Single crochet 3 together) (Insert hook into next st, yo and draw up a lp) in next 3 sts. Yo and draw through all four lps on hook—2 sts dec.

Dishcloth
Bottom Blocks (make 2)
With A ch 2.
Row 1 3 sc in 2nd ch from hook. Ch 1, turn—3 sc.
Row 2 2 sc in 1st sc, sc in each of next 2 sc. Ch 1, turn—4 sc.
Rows 3–12 2 sc in 1st sc, sc in each sc across. Ch 1, turn—14 sc after Row 12.
Row 13 2 sc in 1st sc, sc in each sc across. Change to B, ch 1, turn—15 sc.
Row 14 Sc2tog, sc in each sc across. Ch 1, turn—14 sc.
Rep Row 14 for pattern until 3 sc remain.
Next Row Sc3tog. End off.

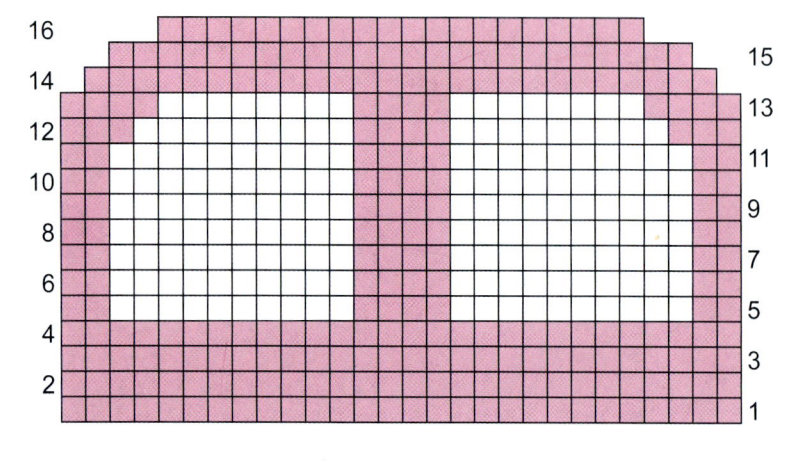

Bottom Block Edging
Work 1 rnd sc evenly spaced around, working A on A sts and B on B sts, placing 3 sc in each corner. Join rnd with sl st in 1st sc. End off.

Assembly
Orient Bottom Blocks so that (B sides) meet at the center front seam as shown in photo, and whip st them together.

Top
Row 1 With C, working across top (B edge) of assembled Blocks, beginning 1 st in from the corner, work 28 sc across, leaving last corner st unworked. Ch 1, turn.
Rows 2–4 Sc in each sc across. Ch 1, turn.
Row 5 Sc in each of 1st 2 sc, with D, sc in each of next 10 sc, with C sc in each of next 4 sc, with D sc in each of next 10 sc, with C, sc in each of last 2 sc. Ch 1, turn.
Rows 6–16 Sc in each sc across following the chart for color changes, and decreasing as shown at beg and end of last 3 rows. End off.

Top Edging
With C, sc evenly spaced across Top. End off.

Tires
First Tire
Row 1 With RS of assembled dishcloth facing, count 3 sts in from right corner and join E with scblo in next sc, scblo in each of next 6 sc. Ch 1, turn.
Rows 2–4 Sc in each sc across, Ch 1, turn.
Row 5 Sc2tog, sc in each of next 3 sc, sc2tog. End off.

Second Tire
Row 1 With RS of assembled dishcloth facing, count 10 sts in from left corner and join E with scblo in that sc, scblo in each of next 6 sc. Ch 1, turn.
Rows 2–5 Rep Rows 2–5 of First Tire.

Headlights (make 2)
With D, ch 2.
Rnd 1 6 sc in 2nd ch from hook.
Rnd 2 2 sc in each sc around. Join rnd with sl st in 1st sc. End off—12 sc.

Finishing
With D, stitch headlights into place as shown on photo.
Weave in ends. ■

Color Key
▨ Color C   ☐ Color D

cupcake cleaner

Yarn
Bernat® Handicrafter® Cotton DeLux™, 5oz/142g skeins, each approx 236yd/215m (cotton)
• 1 skein Espresso #40032 (A)
Lily Sugar 'n Cream Ombres, 2oz/56g skeins, each approx 95yd/86m (cotton)
• 1 skein Pretty Pastels #00199 (B)

Hook
• Size 7 (4.50mm) crochet hook or size needed to obtain gauge

Notions
• Small amount red cotton
• ½"/1.25cm plastic ring
• Tapestry needle

Finished Measurements
9½"/24cm wide at widest point x 8"/20cm tall at tallest point excluding cherry.

Gauge
16 sts and 20 rows to 4"/10cm over scblo.
Take time to check your gauge.

Note
Ch-3 counts as 1 dc throughout.

Stitch Glossary
Scblo Single crochet in the back loop only.

Dishcloth
Cake
With A ch 16.
Row 1 Sc in 2nd ch from hook and in each ch across. Ch 1, turn—15 sc.
Row 2 Scblo in each sc across. Ch 1, turn.
Rep Row 2 for pattern until 26 rows have been completed. End off.

Frosting
With B ch 4 (counts as 1 dc).
Row 1 5 dc in 4th ch from hook. Ch 3, turn—6 dc.
Row 2 Dc in 1st dc, 2 dc in each dc across. Ch 3, turn—12 dc.
Row 3 Dc in 1st dc, dc in next dc, (2 dc in next dc, dc in next dc) 5 times. Ch 3, turn—18 dc.
Row 4 Dc in 1st dc, dc in each of next 2 dc, (2 dc in next dc, dc in each of next 2 dc) 5 times. Ch 3, turn—24 dc.
Row 5 Dc in 1st dc, dc in each of next 3 dc, (2 dc in next dc, dc in each of next 3 dc) 5 times. Ch 3, turn—30 dc.
Row 6 Dc in 1st dc, dc in each of next 4 dc, (2 dc in next dc, dc in each of next 4 dc) 5 times. Ch 3, turn—36 dc.
Row 7 Dc in 1st dc, dc in each of next 5 dc, (2 dc in next dc, dc in each of next 5 dc) 5 times. Ch 1, turn work ¼ turn clockwise—42 dc.

Edging
Row 1 Work 29 sc evenly spaced across straight edge of Top/Frosting. Ch 3, turn.
Row 2 Working in back loop only, 4 dc in 1st sc, *sk 1 sc, sc in next sc, sk 1 sc, 5 dc in next sc. Rep from * to end. End off.

Finishing
With A, sl st top of Base/Cake to front loop of Row 2 of Edging of Top/Frosting. Shell pattern will cover the seam.
With Red, work 16 sc into plastic ring. Join rnd with sl st in 1st sc. End off, leaving long tail with which to sew.
Using tail, sew covered ring to top of Cupcake to serve as a cherry—and a hanger!
Weave in ends.

Paul Amato for Lvarepresents.com

piggy scrubber

Yarn
- Lion Brand® *Kitchen Cotton*, 2oz/57g skeins each approx 99yd/90m (cotton)
- 1 skein Bubble Gum #103

Hook
- Size 7 (4.50mm) crochet hook *or size needed to obtain gauge*

Notions
- Small amounts white and black cotton yarn for eyes
- Pink plastic pot scrubber
- Stitch marker
- Tapestry needle

Finished Measurements
8"/20cm in diameter excluding ears.

Gauge
14 sts and 17 rows to 4"/10cm over sc.
Take time to check your gauge.

Note
Ch-3 counts as 1 dc throughout.

Piggy
Ch 4.
Rnd 1 11 dc in 4th ch from hook. Join rnd with sl st in top of beg-ch—12 dc (ch-3 counts as 1 dc here and throughout).
Rnd 2 Ch 3, dc in 1st dc, 2 dc in each dc around. Join rnd with sl st in top of beg-ch—24 dc.
Rnd 3 Ch 3, dc in 1st dc, dc in next dc, *2 dc in next dc, dc in next dc. Rep from * around. Join rnd with sl st in top of beg-ch—36 dc.
Rnd 4 Ch 3, dc in 1st dc, dc in each of next 2 dc, *2 dc in next dc, dc in each of next 2 dc. Rep from * around. Join rnd with sl st in top of beg-ch—48 dc.
Rnd 5 Ch 3, dc in 1st dc, dc in each of next 3 dc, *2 dc in next dc, dc in each of next 3 dc. Rep from * around. Join rnd with sl st in top of beg-ch—60 dc.
Rnd 6 Ch 3, dc in 1st dc, dc in each of next 4 dc, *2 dc in next dc, dc in each of next 4 dc. Rep from * around. Join rnd with sl st in top of beg-ch—72 dc.
Rnd 7 Ch 3, dc in 1st dc, dc in each of next 5 dc, *2 dc in next dc, dc in each of next 5 dc. Rep from * around. Join rnd with sl st in top of beg-ch. End off—84 dc.

Ears
First Ear
Join yarn with sl st in any dc to start, ch 3.
Row 1 Dc in each of next 4 dc. Ch 3, turn—5 dc.
Row 2 Dc in each dc across. Ch 3, turn.
Row 3 Dc2tog twice. Ch 2, turn.
Row 4 Hdc2tog. End off.

Second Ear
Sk 20 dc after end of Row 1 of First Ear. Join yarn with sl st in next dc, ch 3.
Rep Rows 1–4 of First Ear.

Eyes (make 2)
With white scrap yarn, ch 2.
Rnd 1 6 sc in 2nd ch from hook. Mark 1st st.
Rnd 2 2 sc in each sc around, join with sl st to first sc. End off.

Finishing
With black scrap yarn, embroider snout onto scrubber as shown in photo.
With MC, stitch scrubber into place.
With white scrap yarn, stitch eyeballs into place.
With black scrap yarn, embroider center of each eye with a French knot.
Weave in ends.

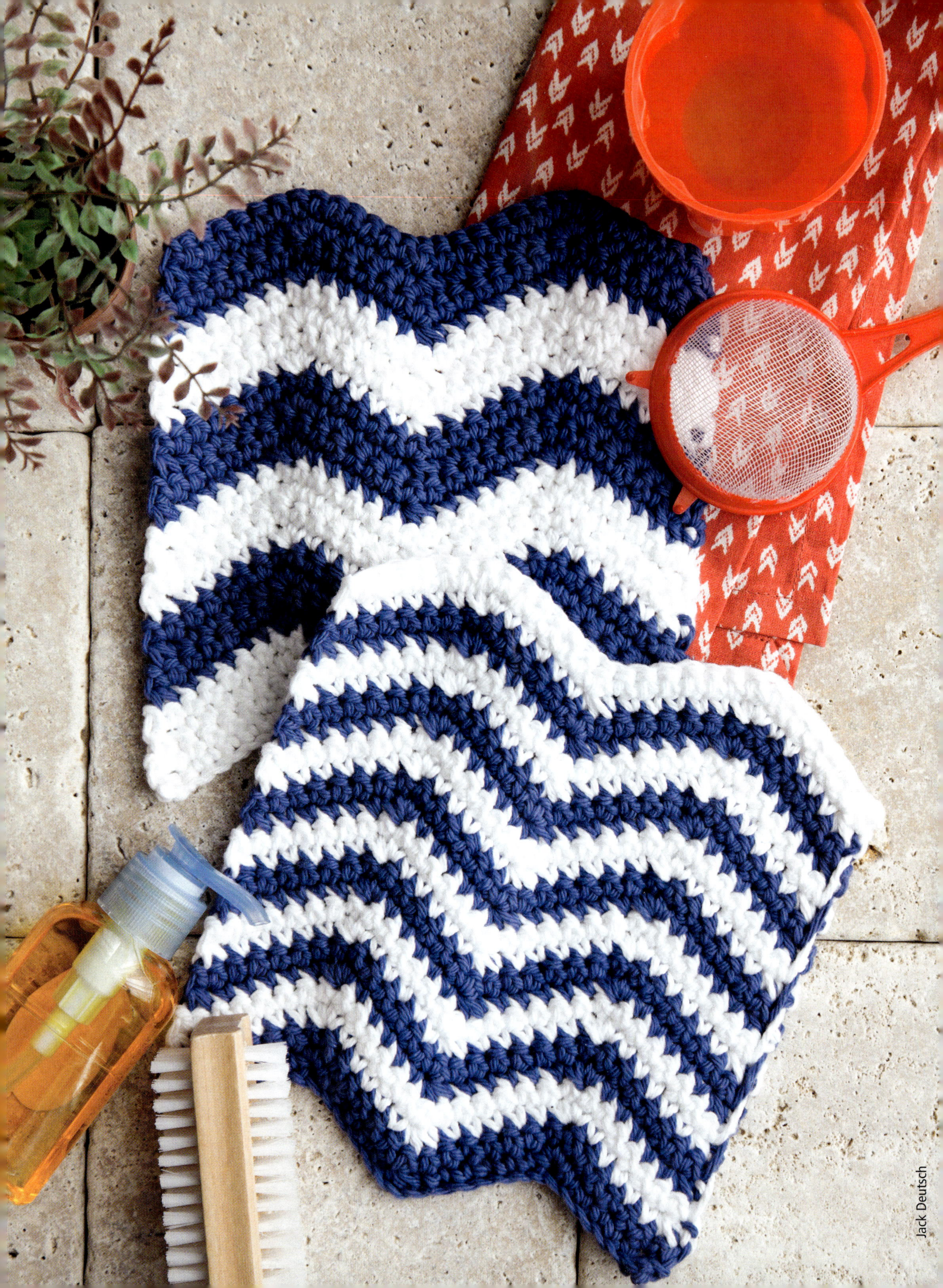

Jack Deutsch

striped chevron dishcloths

Yarn
Bernat® *Handicrafter® Cotton DeLux*™, 5oz/142g balls, each approx 236yd/215m (cotton)
- 1 skein Morning Glory Blue #78108 (A) for both dishcloths

Lily® *Sugar 'n Cream®* Solids, 2½oz/71g balls, each approx 120yd/109m (cotton)
- 1 skein White #102001 (B) for both dishcloths

Hook
- Size H/8 (5mm) crochet hook *or size needed to obtain gauge*

Notions
- Tapestry needle

Finished Measurements
6½"/16.5cm tall x 7"/17.5cm wide.

Gauge
17 sts and 16 rows to 4"/10cm over sc.
Take time to check your gauge.

Stitch Glossary
Sc3tog (Single crochet 3 together) (Insert hook into next st, yo and draw up a lp) in next 3 sts. Yo and draw through all four lps on hook—2 sts dec.

Dishcloth
Chevron Stitch Pattern
Ch 30.
Row 1 Sc2tog in 2nd and 3rd ch from hook, sc 5, 3 sc in next st, sc 5, sc3tog, sc 5, 3 sc in next st, sc 5, sc2tog—29 sc.
Row 2 Sc2tog, sc 5, 3 sc in next st, sc 5, sc3tog, sc 5, 3 sc in next st, sc 5, sc2tog.
Rep Row 2 for 22 more rows—24 rows total.

Wide Stripes Dishcloth
Work chevron stitch pattern as follows:
Using B, ch 30.
*Work 4 rows B.
Work 4 rows A.
Rep from * 3 more times—6 stripes total.
Weave in ends.

Skinny Stripes Dishcloth
Using A, ch 30.
*Work 2 rows A.
Work 2 rows B.
Rep from * 5 more times—12 stripes total.
Weave in ends.

ruffles scrubber

Yarn 4
Lily® Sugar 'n Cream® Ombres, 2oz/56g skeins, each approx 95yd/86m (cotton)
- 1 skein Beach Ball Blue #19316

Hook
- Size 7 (4.50mm) crochet hook *or size needed to obtain gauge*

Notions
- Green plastic pot scrubber
- Stitch marker
- Tapestry needle

Finished Measurements
7½"/19cm in diameter including edging.

Gauge
20 sts and 11 rows to 4"/10cm over sc.
Take time to check your gauge.

Notes
1 First rnd of sc is worked directly into the scrubby by inserting hook down through 2–3 layers of plastic mesh, then up through those layers ¼"/.5cm or so ahead of where the hook went down. Yo, pull through mesh, yo, pull through 2 loops on hook as for regular sc. For extra stability, start each consecutive st by going down into the mesh in the same spot as the previous st came up. Sc will line up side to side around outer edge of scrubber.
2 Crochet is worked in a spiral, mark 1st st of each rnd.

Scrubby
Rnd 1 Work 30 sc evenly spaced around center of scrubby.
Rnds 2–4 Sc in next sc, mark that sc, sc in same sc, 2 sc in each sc around—60 sc after Rnd 2; 240 after Rnd 4.
Rnd 5 Sc in each sc acround.
Rnd 6 Sc in 1st sc, sk 2 sc, 5 dc in next sc, *sk 2 sc, sc in next sc, sk 2 sc, 5 dc in next sc. Rep from * around. Join rnd with sl st in 1st sc. End off.
Weave in ends.

stripy scrubber

Yarn
Lily® *Sugar 'n Cream® Solids*, 2½oz/70g skeins, each approx 120yd/109m (cotton)
- 1 skein Hot Green #01712 (A)

Lily *Sugar 'n Cream Ombres*, 2oz/56 g skeins, each approx 95yd/86m (cotton)
- 1 skein Psychedelic #02600 (B)

Hook
- Size 7 (4.50mm) crochet hook or size needed to obtain gauge

Notions
- Tapestry needle
- Green plastic pot scrubber

Finished Measurements
5½"/14cm in diameter after assembly.

Gauge
14 sts and 14 rows to 4"/10cm over sc.
Take time to check your gauge.

Scrubby
With A ch 33.
Row 1 2 sc in 2nd ch from hook, sc in each of next 29 ch, sc2tog in next ch. Ch 1, turn—32 sc.
Row 2 Sc2tog, sc in each sc across to last sc, 2 sc in last sc. Change to B. Ch 1, turn—32 sc.
Row 3 2 sc in 1st sc, sc in each sc across until 2 sc remain, sc2tog. Ch 1, turn.
Row 4 Sc2tog, sc in each sc across to last sc, 2 sc in last sc. Change to A, ch 1, turn.
Continue on in pattern as established, changing color every 2 rows and keeping increases to one side of the work and decreases to the other, until work measures 18"/45.5cm along one side edge, ending with 2 rows of B.

Assembly
Orient the piece flat on a table so the stripes run from bottom right to top left. The lowest point is on the lower right side; the highest point is on the upper left side. See diagram for additional guidance.
Fold bottom right point (A) up so it meets top right point (B).
Fold top left point (C) down so it meets bottom left point (D).
Pin into place.
Folded Scrubby should look like a square.
With A, whip st seam that runs from C/D to A/B together, being careful not to catch the lower layer of fabric.
Open up the work and turn it on its side—you now have a tube.
With tapestry needle and A, work a running st around top edge of tube. Pull tight to form circle; end off, securing working thread several times.
Rep around bottom edge of tube.
With A, stitch centers together at gathers.
With A, stitch plastic pot scrubber into place at center of one side.
Weave in ends.

Assembly Diagram

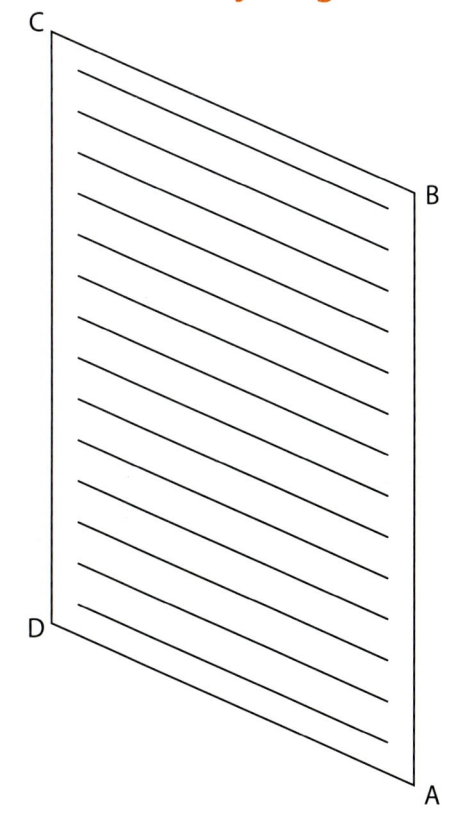

how to change colors

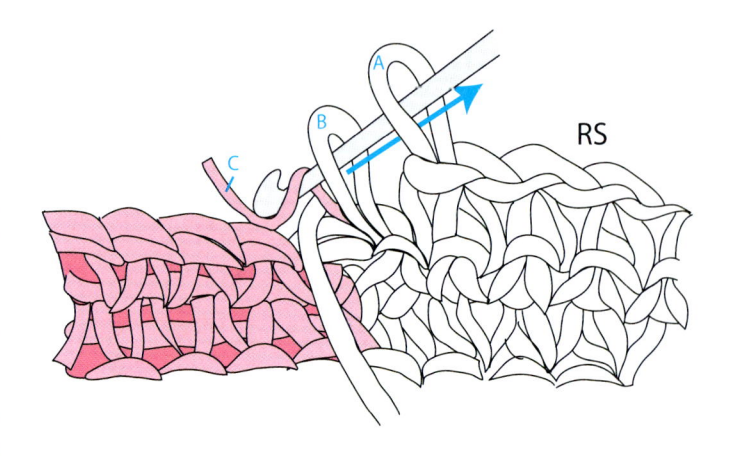

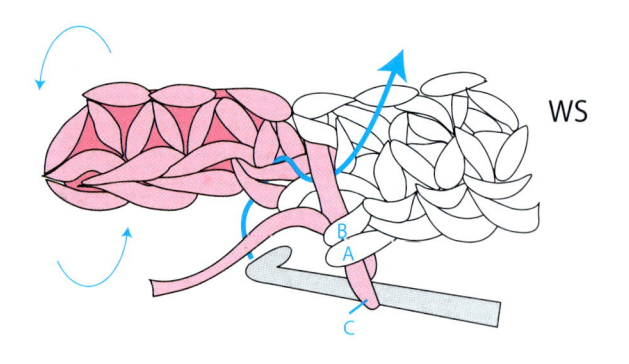

Invisible Float Color Change

The "float" is the created by the new color of yarn traveling from where it is to where you need it to be. It isn't pretty, so this method was devised to hide it! The technique is used when changing from one color to another color in the same row of sc.

Work sc as usual to last sc in old color. (A) Insert hook in st (B), yo, draw through st, bring working yarn to front of work and let it hang for later use, yo with new color (C), draw through two loops on hook (Fig 1).

When woking the first stitch of the new color, insert hook in st and under the float, catching it onto the hook, then yo draw through float and st, yo draw through two loops on hook. Proceed as usual.